Until a few years ago, I was beginning to think I was crazy: wandering the barren Oregon beaches in search of Redtail Surfperch and dredging the jetties for Rockfish well into the night.

Then I met a kindred soul in Ken Hanley. For decades Ken has been tossing flies into the wonderfully varied inshore waters of the California and Baja coasts, pioneering new saltwater fisheries and, perhaps more significantly, stretching the limits of the sport and art of fly angling.

But Ken thought he might be crazy, too. After all, what sane being would brave the pounding surf and the windswept jetties? He was chucking flies into the shoreline salt when tradition dictated that western fly anglers were freshwater folk and, if they were to fish the salt, they'd damn well do it in the warm climes of the equatorial seas.

Ken and I soon discovered a lot of common ground in the methods of our saltwater madness. Our strategies, tactics, tackle and flies offered a case in convergent evolution as we had independently arrived at some very similar ideas about inshore Pacific Coast fly fishing. More importantly, we had arrived at these commonalities because of similar qualities in our attitudes on fly angling – qualities that Ken Hanley possesses in abundance – like a pioneering spirit, a willingness and eagerness to try the untried and to do the undone.

As an instructor, Ken is innovative, gracious, and highly professional. As such, his enthusiasm and excitement permeate this book, tempering all his observations on tackle, technique and locale with an unbounded desire to help others share his world: the world of Pacific Coast inshore fly fishing. Throughout this guide, Ken combines the wisdom of virtually all the pioneering anglers of the Pacific Coast inshore fisheries, to produce a book that cannot help but offer you a new fly fishing challenge. And at the same time introduce you to the insights you will need to succeed at this game.

As Ken says, "This is wild stuff!" And so it is. Easy access, uncrowded, a little exotic, under-appreciated to be sure and just sitting out there waiting: one huge ocean embracing a shoreline that spans the western half of the continent waiting for adventurous anglers to discover its treasures.

Sometimes Ken still wonders whether he might be crazy. Maybe he is. Maybe I am. Maybe anyone willing to explore the vast, thriving beauty of the West Coast, fly rod in hand, is a little crazy. If so – and as this book surely points out – then crazy is something I want to be!

John Shewey
Author, *Trout and Beyond*

A Note from the Author

From the start I've envisioned this project as a workbook for personal observations, to be used much in the same manner as a student's lab journal. The ultimate compliment would be to see my book on your car seat… a "dog-eared, coffee-stained, road-worn journal."

Let's fish for the future and limit our harvest.

Published in 1999 by:
Frank Amato Publications, Inc.
P.O. Box 82112
Portland, Oregon 97282
(503) 653-8108

Softbound UPC: 0-66066-00379-9
Softbound ISBN: 1-57188-177-8

Studio Photography by Guy Gilchrist.
Rear Cover Photo by Greg Jones.
Cover inset photos by the author.
Title Page photo by Terry Baird.
Fly Pattern and Species Illustrations by Barry Glickman.
Tidelog illustrations ©1925 M. C. Escher/Cordon Art-Baarn-Holland

Printed in Canada

10   9   8   7   6   5   4   3   2   1

CONTENTS

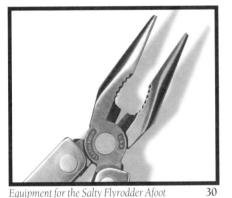

Tides and Moon Phases   15

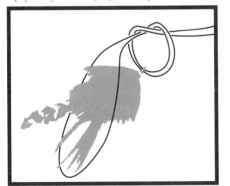

Equipment for the Salty Flyrodder Afoot   30

A Word About Knots and Rigging   34

The Four Micro Habitats   9

The World's a Stage for Fly Fishing...

The Pacific Coast is a true frontier – a place for dreamers and adventurers. It's a land of contrasts, a land of mystery that still captivates our imagination and wanderlust spirit. Shrouded shores and denizens of the deep frequently occupy our fantasies.

The shoreline's images are so keen, they're forever burned in our memory. The delicate sunlight caught in the estuary's aqueous mirror, the roaring surf as it pummels a yielding beachhead, the wind-blown cliffs and bold cypress silhouettes are just a few of these cherished prizes. What a wonderful, even intoxicating, place to be!

The Surf Zone is a treasure house for fly fishers, a place to redefine your fly fishing world. It's challenges are varied; it's rewards are many. The rugged physical features demand versatility in tackle and technique.

Each gamefish has a unique signature. Their strength and ardor is impressive. You'll find celebration in a Perch or Mackerel, just as easily as you'll celebrate a Striped Bass or Corbina.

We've a rich history of pioneering souls that brought fur-n-feathers to our coastal waters. With limited resources and materials, they still had the vision to challenge the limits of tradition. From fly designs to line systems, their impact is a valued legacy to the art of fly fishing. Today's advances in equipment design afford you every opportunity to relish in the sea's bounty.

With virtually thousands of miles of fishable waters, the experience can be tailor-made. You don't need a boat for success here. Fly casting afoot is in many ways an advantage. You can gain access to the most intimate pockets unattainable in any other fashion. The overwhelming enormity of the coastline can be efficiently reduced to personal/private waters. **Just take that first step… there's a lifetime of angling adventure at your beck and call!**

This is an introductory tool to the natural history of your quarry, and the tackle and techniques to ply the Pacific's inshore fisheries. A "rambler's approach," you won't find yourself limited by budget or peripheral equipment.

The Four Micro Habitats

Reducing the sheer immensity of the shoreline environment to manageable subdivisions is key to successful fly fishing afoot. Consider each of the following micro habitats as unique, productive, and approachable with your fly tackle:

- Breakers and Sandy-bottomed Beaches
- Grass-beds and Coves
- Tidepools and Finger Reefs
- Rocky Shores

While you're casting amongst the breakers, it's not always necessary to wade aggressively. Most of the action takes place in water less than four feet deep... thank goodness!

Healthy Coastal Habitat and Common Denominators

To many of the uninitiated, the West Coast's waters impress one as clouded or dirty, lacking the transparent beauty and biological diversity of the South Pacific. This is a misconception. Our West Coast shores are ripe with life.

There is so much life suspended in the water column that it inhibits light from penetrating the depths, creating the unique hues of green and brown found in West Coast waters. Algae, plankton, and countless other microscopic creatures provide the building blocks for a prolific food-chain and sport fishery.

One of the reasons the waters are so productive is that the Pacific seaboard is a somewhat turbulent arena. Wind and current combine to produce an effect known as *coastal upwelling*. The strong offshore winds actually carry the surface waters away, leaving deep, nutrient-rich waters filtering upwards as replacements. Currents alongshore can, and do, produce the same results. This exchange is a key element to supporting the significant bloom of microscopic plants, considered the most important item in the ocean's foodchain... where these plants and organisms thrive *en masse*, foraging fish follow!

When you scrutinize the shoreline, the amazing variety of structure and cover that exists becomes apparent. The larger surf zone and shoreline can be efficiently subdivided into four unique micro habitats: the Breakers and Sandy-bottomed Beaches, Grass-beds and Coves, Tidepools and Finger Reefs, and the Rocky Shoreline (both natural and man-made).

Each of these habitats exhibit a few

Tidepools can vary in size and depth but one thing's for certain, they're a challenging maze with fish holding tight to cover.

key common denominators. They're dramatically affected by tide and current, and they all represent a locale where ocean and land become one. They are places in flux, and that's to their credit. The transformations are both subtle and abrupt, at times tumultuous, even treacherous. It's a perpetual drama – seasonal, daily, and hourly by Nature's eminent design. Although these various niches are teeming with wildlife, most of the sportfish populations here are generally transient and free roaming with the changing tides.

Most successful flyfishers begin an outing by observing first and casting second. Take the time to interpret your surroundings. Look for what field naturalists refer to as "breaking zones." Anglers commonly call these mini-zones "edges." Breaking zones

"I decided that the best thing I could do for my coastal fly fishing technique was to leave the tackle at home! A pencil and paper were going to be far more valuable to me. Decades later I'm still recording my observations, swapping ideas with other shoreline pioneers, and the refinements have produced a ton of fish on the fly!"

are those environmental edges where change occurs: light to dark, deep to shallow, open water to thick cover,

warm to cold, and so on. Fish use these edges for movement, feeding, and concealment. As you become more adept at recognizing these important zones, you'll find that you've also become more successful as a salty shoreline flyfisher.

The Breakers and Sandy-Bottomed Beach

Breakers are the waves that build and collapse the beach environment. The more violent the wave action, the greater the eroding effects, eventually pulling sand toward deeper water beyond the visible surfline. Milder curling waves actually carry the sand back toward shore, rebuilding the beachhead and starting the cycle anew. The winter months typically find the beach being reduced, while the summer cycle rejuvenates the habitat.

Footing can be tricky along the rocky shore. In this "industrial strength" habitat, heavier tackle is the name of the game.

When it comes to approachable water, it's pretty hard to beat an open beachfront. Actual property sizes vary, from miles of uninterrupted flats to small private beaches no more than fifty yards long.

Learning to "read the water" here is critical. Just as you'd learn the visual keys to your favorite trout stream, the surfline affords great visual support in narrowing down where the action might take place. The basic elements to work with include wave structure, current seams, and beach topography.

Wave structure is by far the easiest element to observe, and probably the most reliable. Essentially you'll be looking for the changes in wave height. The more radical the change, the greater the relevance in identifying a breaking zone.

As the wave travels over, or comes

"… underwater observations became invaluable. Just confirming fish were in the area was enough to boost our confidence to cast a fly. Knowing how fish were hugging a rocky holdfast, or schooling along a sandy spit, gave us the edge we needed. These first-hand experiences subsurface were the catalyst to my salty flyrodding pursuits."

in contact with shallow obstacles, the tide's energy is absorbed by creating drag and wave build-up. The shallow-

er the terrain, the higher the wave's crest. Deeper obstacles allow the tide's energy to be dissipated over a larger area. The end result leaves calmer seas at the top of the water column. Everything is relative, don't ask how high the wave should be, but rather how notable is the difference between it's crest and sloping edges. Often the crest sports a frothy, foaming look. As your eyes scan sideways down the crest, note where the wave begins to disappear. You've just identified a meaningful change in the topography of the beach; a breaking zone from shallow to deeper structure.

As the rolling surf transports and recycles sand particles from the sea floor and shore, it creates a series of bars as it approaches the shallows. The most conspicuous feature you'll notice is commonly referred to as a *trough*.

Many inshore species favor the protected grass beds as prime spawning grounds.

another. The stronger currents will provide a greater concentration of suspended food, similar to current seams in a river, or wind seams on a lake's surface. It's prime property for casting your fly.

Additionally, *pockets* and *cuts* are two more important aspects to the topography of the beach. They're usually found in relationship to scattered rock formations, or man-made habitat, like pilings. This natural maze reduces the heavy blows of current and tide. Softer, swirling, back-eddies provide protection for smaller species.

Pools are another prime feature to work with. Watch the water as it recedes from the sandy beach. Anywhere you see standing water you've identified a pool. Look down the beach and make note of any high sandy peninsulas. The more prominent the high point, the larger the pool potential and "school potential!" The surf scouring against the pool's walls, creates a tremendous feeding zone.

The Pacific mole crab, marine worms, soft-shelled clams, baitfish and the fry of gamefish are the foremost items in the foodchain. You're likely to encounter an impressive variety of game within the breakers. From quarter pound dynamos to multi-pound marauders, you can pursue several types of surfperch, smelt, striped bass, flounder, corbina, and more. The farther south, the wider the variety of species encountered.

Grass-beds and Coves

With the exception of tidal action and wave surge, grass-beds and coves are the inshore version of a small alpine lake. Yesterday, smooth as glass. Today, a frothy wind whipped surface.

Running parallel to the shore, it's the flattened water between the sandbars and each set of waves. You can consider troughs as highways for both predator and prey species moving within the breakers.

Look to the surface and note the foam and flotsam. You'll see in some areas where it tends to raft in a narrow corridor. Watch to see if it is actually being drawn out to sea in the same configuration. If so, you've identified a significant feature we call a *channel* or *rip*. Channels run perpendicular to the shore, providing entry and exit lanes for fish to travel from one trough to

Tomorrow, who knows?

Each day the semi-protected cove will partially fill and empty as the tide dictates. During lower water levels seize the opportunity to gaze into the intricate cover where you'll present your fly. This mini-habitat with its sheltered nature, fosters the growth of sea grasses and mixed algae. It's a forest of wondrous gifts for the fish, and of course, ultimately, you the flyfisher.

Thick patches of surfgrass or eelgrass provide shelter and sustenance to entire foodchains. Snails and herring eggs cling to the slender blades. Small crustaceans crawl within the canopy and along the grass base. Baitfish dart and hover among the gently swaying cover. The seagrass are a rich and vibrant community that beg your angling attention.

Field observations in these waters parallel that of a stillwater flyfisher in the High Sierra. Concentrate on cruising lanes, rather than holding lies. The edges of weed carpets, rocky outcroppings, ledges and shelves, all become byways for entry and exit into cover. Most fish entering the cove don't have the luxury of bedding down for any extended period of time. The few that do will be virtually impossible to coax onto your fly.

Identify schooling activity by watching cormorants, grebes and other diving birds. Sounding sea lions are also a key indicator of fish populations in the cove. Sighting jumping baitfish is a sure-fire indicator of a predator pushing prey.

Tidepools and Finger Reefs
The tidepool and finger reef are possibly the most exotic and demanding inshore fishery you'll come across.

Finger reefs might best be described as narrow-walled corridors and sandy-bottomed shore. Their long tendrils are composed of hard rock and sediment. Often they radiate from the tidepools nearby, and have the same composition.

> *Many of the species highlighted in the inshore environment can be found in more than one of the micro habitats (increasing their appeal to the fly game). Extra incentive exists here for a "once-in-a-lifetime" catch.* **It's exotic, wild, and challenging. It doesn't get any better than this!**

"Stalking" comes to mind whenever I think of this unique opportunity afoot. Short, precise casts into cover are the norm. Consider this "ambush" property as holding lies dominate the rampart. This is wicked country on your terminal tackle. The rock is sharp, the water is littered, and there are any number of creatures that could munch your leader and fly. Razor-sharp teeth and pincers abound in this menagerie. I've been broken off more than a few times by a surprise siege from a monkeyface eel.

Don't be led astray by your first thoughts; this isn't just angling to tiny aquarium sized fish like gobies, sculpins, and blennies. (Although they can be great fun on a four-weight

outfit!) You could find yourself working your fly in a pool ten feet deep, or swimming it through a mere ten inches of water. Depending on the topography, you just might be standing near a real bruiser. It's wild stuff!

Explore every pocket, undercut, and surge channel. With such superb camouflage don't expect to actually see many fish. This is instinctive territory. When in doubt… make the cast.

On rare occasions you can view tailing quarry. Usually your highest success will come from working tight to the reef's wall. This arena is home to species like spotfin croaker, greenling, grass rockfish, buffalo sculpin, perch and more. The fish here find the bulk of their diet consists of small invertebrates, crustaceans, and algae.

Rocky Shoreline
If you haven't got a sandy beach in your home waters, you surely have rocky habitat. The rocky shore occurs both as a natural phenomenon and man-made structure. Battered by relentless wave surge and current, it bears witness to the sea's magnificent power. Wind and water are the dominant tools sculpting the rock and clay. The exposed coastline is cut, shattered, ground down, and polished. Definitely "industrial-strength" habitat!

Anything could be lurking in the depths, ready to strike at a moments notice. Nowhere else in the inshore realm are the relationships of predator and prey so dramatic.

Naturally occurring formations may appear inaccessible. Plunging cliffs not withstanding, there's usually access. On closer inspection the rock's craggy character may soon reveal a pathway leading to a prime casting station. Perhaps a tiny promontory, or terrace. Sometimes you can stroll right up to position. Other situations demand the artful skills of a rock-climber. Some access points will have you casting straight out to sea, while others will put you over private waters known as *pocket pools*.

Pocket pools are coveted ground, protected from the sea's torrent by dense jungles of giant kelp and rocky pillars. Like a private sanctuary, the pool's water hosts numerous species. Fish hover along the *stipes* (stems) of the kelp, or seek protection under the profuse canopy that's buoyed by gas-filled bulbs.

Breakwaters and jetties are man-made structures usually associated with a harbor's entryway. They often exist near the mouth of bays, estuaries, and sloughs. Their rip-rap features draw a host of gamefish that readily attack a fly. This "built" environment is generally much easier to negotiate on foot than Mother Nature's complex counterpart.

There's usually a distinct difference between the water's characteristics on either side of the bulwark. Seaside, the habitat is fully engaged in the wave surge of the tide. Along the inner wall you'll experience a calmer, more consistent environment. Each side of the structure offers unique challenges in capturing the variety of available species. Both sides are worth the effort.

The astonishing medley of inshore species continues to grow within the rocky shoreline; Pacific bonito, cabezon, rubberlip and pile perch, Pacific tomcod, jacks, sargo and opaleye. The list goes on and on…

Tides and Moon Phases

The ability to read a tide chart is one of the premier skills needed for successful saltwater flyrodding. The information you glean from this document will undoubtedly dictate when and where you choose to cast a fly.

The Importance of Recognizing Moon Phases

The Moon and the Sun's combined influence on our ocean's water mass is extraordinary. Their gravitational control creates the rising and dropping of the water column.

The Moon's influence is the most important aspect to consider as a field tool for fly fishing. For a quick reference to potential tide conditions on any given day, check the Moon's phase. The tide is directly related to the cycle of the Moon: from the *full* Moon phase, continuing through the wane into the *new* Moon, and starting the cycle anew with the *waxing* phase again.

The strongest tides, those exhibiting extreme highs (flood) and lows (ebb), correspond to the New and Full Moon phases. These two tides are referred to as "spring tides."

Weaker, more moderate tides are experienced during the *quarter* Moon phases. They're commonly known as "neap tides." The shoreline is notably calmer during this time in the month.

Following the lunar cycle, spring tides and neap tides occur on opposite weeks. Once you identify the first spring tide, simply look to every other week and predict a similar tide.

Since the Moon rises later each day, by approximately fifty minutes, the tides exhibit a corresponding time shift. If today's morning low occurred at 6:00 a.m., you can anticipate tomorrow's low tide around 7:00 in the morning.

So, Just What is the Best Time to Fly Fish?

No single tide can claim the "magic window" for the entire West Coast. There are too many variables to consider. Slope profile, bottom cover, wind exposure – all are examples of the numerous important factors we have to consider when choosing angling locations. Here are a few general rules to get started:

1. To get a first-hand look at the topography of any beachhead, consider the low during a spring tide. At this time you're more likely to see exposed ridges, pools, steep or shallow slopes, and various cover that would be submerged during any other tide phase.

2. Neap tides create a more stable environment around any rocky habitat. From peak low, to peak high, there's very little change in the environment. Sportfish populations are likely to take advantage of the higher water column to rest, roam, and feed among the rocks and cover.

Knowing when the incoming tide occurs can make all the difference in the world.

Courtesy of Pacific Publishers, Bolinas, California
Tidelog illustrations by M. C. Escher, "Second Day of Creation," ©1925 M. C. Escher/Cordon Art-Baarn-Holland

3. As the tide rises, it will generally bring to shore a variety of food items found in slightly deeper water. This shift in the foodchain (including plankton, baitfish, etc.) helps to establish a prime feeding zone within the shallows. The tide's added scouring against the rocks and sandy shoreline exposes small crustaceans, marine worms, mollusks, and other food items to the mix.

Whenever possible, take the time to walk a site, first, before you try your fly tackle in the same environment. The insights gained from a pre-fly fishing outing will help you quickly advance "up the learning curve." You'll have a clearer picture when matching your tackle to the habitat and species. Your field technique will automatically refine itself as you spend more time on the water.

Timing Your Tide To Local Quirks

Imagining that there's a difference between the beachhead along Washington's Olympic Peninsula and Baja's northern seaboard isn't so hard. Taking it a step further and imagining that there's a difference between

beaches just two to five miles apart might be a bit more difficult, but it's the more significant observation to work with. One beach might "jump start" at the beginning of the tide, while neighboring locales might

Please Take Note:

Tidetables are "educated predictions." They are less accurate during periods of offshore storms, strong Spring Tides, etc. Just the same, they are the best tool at our disposal for gaining insights to potentially prime fishing conditions.

require more water movement before any angling action kicks in. If the sandy shore you're standing on has a rather abrupt drop to it, you might opt to work the first few hours of tide. If the beachhead has a mild profile, you might want to wait until the tide

floods the shallows, opting to work the last half of the rising tide plus the beginning of the out-going phase.

One observation that seems to get a thumbs-up from every salty flyrodder is that moving water is essential to success. Slack periods (peak high and peak low) just don't offer the gamefish enough incentives to keep active. *Remember, you're trying to key into feeding cycles which are more likely to occur when the tide stirs up the mix.*

Adjustments

Since our coastline isn't just a straight line from north to south, you'll notice that your tide chart will require adjustments to fine-tune the prediction for a specific location. You'll be required to either add or subtract minutes from the data presented. Most tide charts provide a comprehensive listing of locations with tide corrections. The adjustments available account for both the time and the height of the tide.

For those of you who prefer working the harbor and jetty environments, another valued piece of information is knowing the current's speed. Again, your tide chart may provide you with the appropriate statistics to make adjustments for your specific region.

West Coast Species Sampler

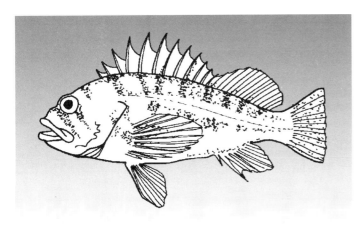

ROCKFISH

Black, Copper, Blue, and Olive Rockfish are the most common catch for the inshore fly fisher. These fish favor shallow, rocky habitat including breakwaters, rocky shoreline, kelp beds, and soft bottomed environments.

They're "bass-like" in appearance with short thick bodies, large surfaced fins, and powerful broom tails. They're well-suited to work within tight cover. Spawning takes place in the shallows from November through March. The rockfish diet varies from baitfish and small crustaceans, to squid, clams, and marine worms.

Fly Selection and Field Tips
- Gold Buccaneer
- Purple Eelworm
- Salty Seafoam Blonde
- Foam or Hard-bodied Popper
- Best opportunities are at night during quarter moon phases
- Try working the incoming tide

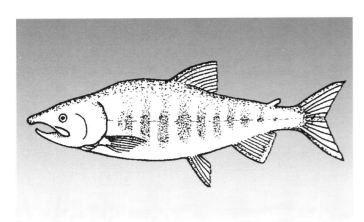

CHUM SALMON

The Fall Season offers us an opportunity for "salty salmon"... the oyster beds off Puget Sound play host to chum arriving during the spawn. Peak runs for this unique fishery occur from September well into November. Like other Pacific salmon, chum are driven into fresh water by the urge to spawn.

As they travel farther up-river food is often the last thing on their mind. However, while they're still in any saltwater environs they will frequently inhale a fly.

Fly Selection and Field Tips
- Chum Candy, Chartreuse
- Chum Candy, Hot Pink
- Shewey's Kilchis Killer
- Floating line, long leader (9–12 feet)
- Don't over-animate the retrieve
- The strike is usually very subtle
- Be prepared for a "hot" fresh-run fish

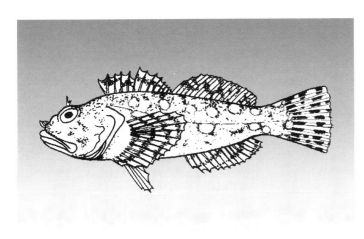

CABEZON

"Cabs" are a member of the sculpin family. They reside in most rocky habitats (including tidepools). Their elongate bodies afford access to the narrowest of shelters. Large pectoral fins help them hug bottom cover.

Spawning occurs inshore, and usually peaks during December and January. They aggressively guard their nests.

Cabezon have an unusually large mouth compared to the rest of their body. Their favorite edibles are crabs and small fish.

Fly Selection and Field Tips
- Lefty's Deceiver, Olive
- Labyrinth Crab
- Sasquatch (Dark)
- Best opportunities are at night
- Strictly fish the bottom
- Move the fly s-l-o-w-l-y
- High Density Head (400+ grains)

West Coast Species Sampler

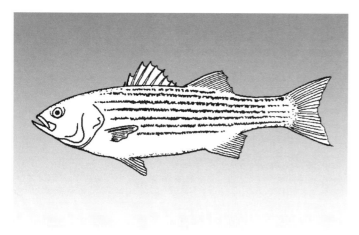

STRIPED BASS

Stripers are one of the most celebrated inshore gamefish. They were brought to us from the Eastern Shoreboard in 1879. During early Spring they spawn in fresh water, then venture into the saltchuck from late Spring through the entire summer season. They roam the surfline and rocky shore looking to bulk-up on Anchovies and other easy pickings. There's nothing subtle about their feeding demeanor in saltwater.

This is a powerful full-sized fish with a fairly streamlined profile.

Fly Selection and Field Tips
- Large Poppers, White or Black
- Sar-Mul-Mac, Mullet version
- Black Bonzai
- Best chance off of rocky points during quarter moon phases
- Floating line with poppers (p.m.)
- Streamers best with shooting head (200–300 grains), stout leader (4–6 feet)

SURFPERCH

Barred, Redtail, and Walleye Surfperch dominate the breakers and sandy-bottomed beach. Striped, pile, and rainbow perch favor the rocky shore and/or man-made structure.

Most of the species breed in the late fall and winter. Spawning uccurs during the spring into early summer. The prime zone for targeting these little dynamos ranges from one to four feet deep.

They consume the Pacific mole crab, shrimp, marine worms, and tiny baitfish.

Fly Selection and Field Tips
- Screamin' (Shad) Shrimp
- Surfpercher Red
- Shad Fly, Silver/Red
- Phillips' Krab Kreature
- Sink tip or shooting heads (200–400 grains), short leaders (3–6 feet)
- Fish near the bottom first
- Better to work numerous short casts (approx. 35–50 feet)

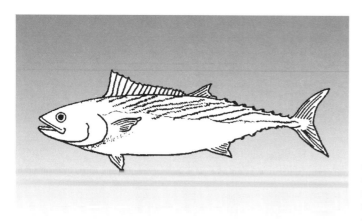

PACIFIC BONITO

"Boneheads" are members of the mackerel and tuna family, hence the beautiful hydro-dynamic profile.

The protected waters of California's southern bays offer the best opportunity for fly fishing afoot. Water temperature plays an important role here; the fish will seek warmer water.

Locations with commercial bait receivers are prime... these fish are constantly looking to fuel the fire.

Bonito dine primarily on anchovies and small baitfish.

Fly Selection and Field Tips
- Blanton's Fatal Attraction
- Clouser's Deep Minnow, White
- Wayfarer
- Pearl Yeti
- Shooting heads or sink tip (300–400 grains), short leaders (2–4 feet)
- Work from surface to 30 feet deep
- Be prepared for strong/fast runs

West Coast Species Sampler

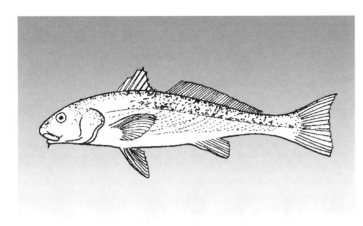

CORBINA

Probably the toughest inshore gamefish to catch on the Pacific Coast! An ancient looking fish, they have a very small mouth positioned almost directly underneath the head. Their single chin barbel is a sensory device probably used to help detect food buried in the sand. They feed extensively on sand crabs (Pacific mole).

Corbina frequent the surfline and sandy-bottomed shore. They're often found cruising in just inches of water. Peak season in the surf occurs throughout the summer, especially July and August.

Fly Selection and Field Tips
- Phillips' Krab Kreature
- Mini Puff, Orange
- Sight fishing to individuals
- Cast after the surf rolls in
- The fish's take is subtle, wait before you set the hook
- Floating head or sink tip line

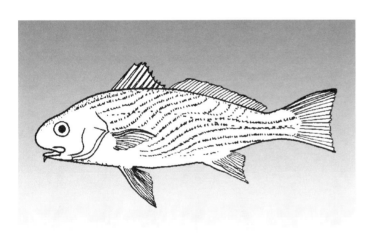

CROAKER

Both Yellowfin and Spotfin Croaker are abundent in the sandy-bottomed surf and protected bays. Prime time in the shallows takes place throughout the summer months. Look for them in waters less than five feet deep. They're a fish that runs in moderately sized schools.

The croaker's diet consists of baitfish, shrimp, sand crabs, marine worms, and clams.

They seem to travel to deeper waters during the colder months.

Fly Selection and Field Tips
- Screamin' (Shad) Shrimp
- Shad Fly, Silver and Red
- Clouser Minnow, White
- Fish the incoming tide
- Sink tip or shooting heads (200–400 grains), short leaders (3–6 feet)

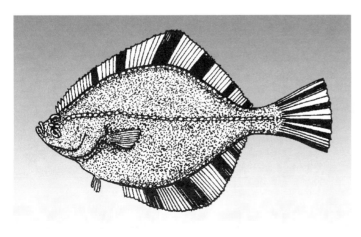

FLATFISH

Starry Flounder and California Halibut are the two most commonly encountered "flatties" for the fly fisher. Both of these species prefer shallow sandy habitat.

Starry flounder can be found in surf, sloughs, and estuaries. Halibut will most likely be found along the surfline.

The Halibut prefers to eat anchovies and sardina, while the smaller flounder consumes crustaceans and marine worms primarily. Most flatfish are aggressive predators.

Fly Selection and Field Tips
- Pink Keel Bugger
- Gold Buccaneer
- Labyrinth Crab
- High density head (400+ grains)
- Strictly fish the bottom
- Short, stout leaders (2–4 feet)
- Creep and twitch the fly slowly

West Coast Species Sampler

SAND BASS

Both Barred and Spotted "sandies" provide great opportunities for inshore flyrodding. Spotted sand bass frequent the protected waters of estuaries and bays, while barred sandies can be found among the rocks, kelp, and surfline.

Spawning season brings the sand bass into the shallows. Prime months occur from May through September. Their diet consists primarily of crustaceans and baitfish.

Fly Selection and Field Tips
- Labyrinth Crab
- Wayfarer
- Lefty's Deceiver
- Cast close to any cover, especially pilings, rocks, and eelgrass beds
- The night bite can be tremendous
- Work with sinking style lines, medium length leaders (6–9 feet)

LINGCOD

Lings are a tough fish. Their toothy maw and aggressive nature has given rise to nick names like "Seawolf" and "Dragon-of-the-Sea." The adult lingcod's diet centers on baitfish, while the young ling dines on shrimp and crabs.

They spawn in the shallows during the winter season. The males are aggressive while guarding the nest.

Lingcod prefer rocky habitat. They hug bottom cover. You can't be afraid of losing a fly. If you're not snagging on bottom cover… you're not getting your fly in front of a lingcod!

Fly Selection and Field Tips
- Black Bonzai
- Gold Buccaneer
- Purple Eelworm
- High-density head (400+ grains), short leaders (2– 4 feet), add a short shock trace of wire for the tippet

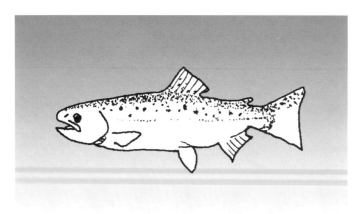

SILVER SALMON

Silvers, also known as Coho Salmon, are a top fighting gamefish in the salt.

Coho will most likely be caught along jetties and estuary mouths on their way to freshwater spawning beds. The spawning cycle takes place during Fall and into early Winter.

The salmon prefer to eat baitfish while in the open sea. They're in transition while in the estuary environment and eating begins to take on less importance, yet they can still exhibit aggressive behavior as they gear up for the spawn.

Fly Selection and Field Tips
- Fatal Attraction
- Wayfarer
- Lefty's Deceiver
- High-density head (300+ grains), medium stout leaders (4–6 feet)
- Work surface to 15 feet deep
- Work the fly aggressively

Fly Pattern Recipes and Angling Tips

Tied by John Shewey

BLACK BONZAI

Created by John Shewey, this fly was designed for fooling those denizens of the shoreline; such as cabezon and lingcod.

The pattern is best presented with a high density shooting head and very short leader. Move the fly with a long, slow stripping technique. Be sure to let the fly pause between strips. On occasion a short quick dart might draw attention.

Work the Bonzai in deep pocket pools, off rocky breakwaters, and along any finger reef environment.

Materials
- Hook: Standard saltwater, #1/0–5/0
- Thread: Black
- Tail: Black saddle 10–12, Black Krystal Flash
- Body: Black rabbit strip, 2 strips Gold mylar on each side
- Topping: Black Krystal Flash, full
- Eyes: Optional, lead barbell

Commercial production tie

BLANTON'S SAR-MUL-MAC

A classic saltwater pattern from Dan Blanton, developed in the 70's. It can readily be adapted to imitate a sardine, mullet, or mackerel. It provides a full-bodied profile with enticing action.

Consider using the fly with a Homer Rhodes or Duncan style loop. The added action can be a real trigger. Striped bass and any large predator will respond to the fly.

Materials
- Hook: Standard saltwater, #1/0–4/0
- Thread: White
- Tail: White bucktail
- Underwing: 6–9 White saddle hackle, Silver Flashabou
- Overwing: White bucktail, 1 Grizzly hackle each side
- Collar: Red chenille
- Eyes: Glass doll, solid 6–8mm
- Head and Topping: White chenille, Gray chenille or herl on top

Tied by the author

BLANTON'S FATAL ATTRACTION

Dan Blanton created this original design for taking Pacific bonito in Southern California's King's Harbor. The pattern has since found wide appeal as a general attractor for numerous inshore species.

Present the fly with a series of erratic moves, darting and dipping as if it were an injured baitfish. Vary the length and cadence of your retrieve. It's a great choice to imitate anchovies or sardines.

Materials
- Hook: Standard Saltwater, #2–1/0
- Thread: White
- Eyes: Medium bead chain
- Tail: Silver Flashabou
- Body: Pearl braided mylar
- Collar: Large White saddle, folded
- Wing: Layered – White bucktail, Blue bucktail, Pearl Krystal Flash, topped with peacock herl

Fly Pattern Recipes and Angling Tips

Tied by the author

CHUM CANDY

This candy was created specifically for the chum salmon roaming Washington's oyster beds.

The pattern is simplicity at its finest. A touch of color here, a bit of flash there, and presto… you've got a trigger for fish to strike.

The Chartreuse version seems to receive more strikes during a season, however, a pink alternate is often the ticket when the Salmon have lock-jaw.

Using a floating line and long leader, animate the fly with a series of short strips.

Materials
- Hook: Salmon/Steelhead, #2–6
- Thread: Fluorescent Green floss
- Tail: Tying thread
- Body: Tying thread
- Wing: Green Krystal Flash, sparse profile
- The alternate version uses Fluorescent Pink floss, Pink Krystal Flash

Commercial production tie

CLOUSER'S DEEP MINNOW

A remarkable generic pattern created by Bob Clouser. This little streamer has been so effective in a wide variety of saltwater environs, it's truly become a "must have" for most salty flyrodders.

The pattern is a super choice to imitate any small baitfish. Numerous color combinations can be effective.

Wether you're using a sinking or floating style line, animate the fly with a crippled look. Take advantage of the "jigging action" inherent in the pattern's design.

Materials
- Hook: Standard saltwater, #2–6
- Thread: Gray or Silver
- Eyes: Lead barbell, painted Red withBlack pupils
- Throat: White bucktail
- Wing: Silver Krystal Flash topped with Gray or White bucktail

Tied by the author

GOLD BUCCANEER

This fly is the author's conception to entice any bottom feeding species. Rockfish and small flatfish, especially starry flounder, have eaten the fly regularly. The rockfish and "flatties" respond best during a night bite.

Present the fly on a high density shooting head with very short leader. Use a slow seductive uninterrupted retrieve.

Materials
- Hook: Standard Saltwater, #2–2/0
- Thread: Fluorescent Yellow floss
- Tail/Antennae: White Bucktail
- Tip: Fluorescent Yellow floss
- Eyes: Lead or large bead chain
- Wing: Peacock Krystal Flash, Gold Flashabou
- Body: (change to standard thread) Lite Brite Yellow, apply with dubbing loop
- Collar: Saddle hackle, 1 Yellow, 1 Orange, 1 Yellow large webbed

Fly Pattern Recipes and Angling Tips

Tied by the author

KILCHIS KILLER

Here's John Shewey's tempter for the chum salmon of the Kilchis River in Oregon. This fly has also proven itself as a success in the saltwater fishery around Washington's Hood Canal.

Chartreuse color schemes are the standard among chum salmon offerings, and that's true no matter where you present your fly.

Using a floating line and long leader, animate the fly with a series of short, subtle strips. Salty chum are a hot fish. Be prepared for a strong and feisty opponent.

Materials
- Hook: Heavy wire, Gold, #2–6
- Thread: Chartreuse floss
- Tail: Chartreuse Krystal Flash
- Body: Half tying thread, half chartreuse cactus chenille
- Wing: Chartreuse Krystal Flash
- Collar: Chartreuse hackle

Tied by the author

LABYRINTH CRAB

Designed by the author. This simple pattern can be done in any color combination to imitate shore crabs, rock crabs, or porcelain crabs. The pattern gets down quickly and the materials give it a great lively action.

Work the fly around any rocky habitat, among seaweed, grass-beds, tidepools and estuaries. You can't worry about losing your fly… just carry along some extras!

Materials
- Hook: Saltwater long, #1/0–2
- Weight: Wire along top shank
- Thread: Tan or Brown
- Butt: Small ball of Fluorescent Orange chenille
- Claws: Pheasant tail on bottom, Grizzly hackle tips on top
- Rear Hackle: Grizzly
- Body: Bleached opossum
- Collar: Most any soft hackle

Tied by Larry Kovi

LEFTY'S DECEIVER, OLIVE

From the imagination of Lefty Kreh came one of the most celebrated patterns in saltwater (and freshwater for that matter)… the Deceiver Series. Lefty's favorite color scheme is the olive design. Now you can't get a better recommendation than that.

Use this pattern anytime it calls for an aggressive predator/prey situation. An erratic and lively retrieve works wonders.

Materials
- Hook: Standard Saltwater, #2–2/0
- Thread: Green
- Tail: 6–12 White saddle hackle, 1 Olive-dyed Grizzly on each side, Olive or Gold Krystal Flash accent
- Body: Green diamond braid
- Beard: Red Krystal Flash
- Collar: White bucktail, small bunch top and bottom of shank
- Topping: Yellow bucktail sparse, 10–15 Peacock herl
- Head: Tying thread, eyes optional

Fly Pattern Recipes and Angling Tips

Tied by the author

MINI PUFF

First winning its reputation as a superb bonefish pattern, the Puff has a unique role on the West Coast… imitating the roe sac of our favorite sand crab. This orange version is a dead ringer for the crab's brilliant colored eggs.

Sportfish in the surf (corbina, croaker, and surfperch) key in on the delectable Pacific mole crab (*Emerita analoga*). It's number one in their diets.

Keep your fly close to the bottom, the sand crab is a very weak swimmer.

Materials
- Hook: Standard Saltwater, #4–6
- Thread: Orange
- Eyes: Small bead chain, or lead barbell for deep/heavy surf
- Wing: Brown calftail, 2 Grizzly hackle tips outward
- Head: Fluorescent Orange chenille

Tied by the author

PEARL YETI

Hatched by the author, the Yeti is a solid choice to imitate any small baitfish; especially pinhead anchovy, candlefish, and smelt fry. Bonito, mackerel, topsmelt, and surface roaming rockfish eat the fly.

The pattern is most effective near the surface or at depths of less than twenty feet. Work the fly with a series of short and long strips. Using your rod tip, redirect the fly's course every so often, as if it were bait fleeing danger.

Materials
- Hook: Salmon/Steelhead, #2–4
- Thread: White
- Tag: Fluorescent Green floss
- Butt: Tying thread
- Tail: Poly yarn
- Body: Lite Brite, Pearl Blue, apply with dubbing loop
- Collar: Teal flank
- Wing: White calftail

Tied by Britt Phillips

PHILLIPS' KRAB KREATURE

Britt Phillips intended this fly to fool primarily surfperch. He says the pattern is a stepchild of sorts, his inspiration coming from Andy Burk's freshwater Dragon Bugger.

Use this salty version anytime you're working the sandy shoreline. It's an excellent imitation of the Pacific mole crab. You can weight the pattern with either lead eyes, or lead wire wrapped around the shank.

Materials
- Hook: Saltwater keel, #4–6
- Thread: Tan or Gray
- Roe Sac: Orange Glo Bug yarn
- Tail: Tan Elk (upright, sparkle dun style), top with Grizzly marabou
- Eyes: Plastic bead chain
- Body: Tan or Gray leech yarn
- Head: Spun wool, dubbing loop
- Shell: Hot glue stick. Use soapy water on your fingers to mold the glue shell and body.

Fly Pattern Recipes and Angling Tips

Tied by John Shewey

PINK KEEL BUGGER

This pattern is a strong imitation for mud shrimp and marine worms. It was created by John Shewey for the starry flounder and inshore fishery of Oregon and Washington.

Your presentation will call for a high density sinking shooting line. Short leaders will help keep the fly under control. Animate the fly with slow, short strips. Make numerous casts to cover an entire area.

Work the fly in sandy-bottomed habitat near jetties, finger reefs, coves, and the surfline.

Materials
- Hook: Saltwater keel, #2–6
- Thread: Red or Pink
- Tail: Shell Pink marabou, Magenta Flashabou
- Body: Shell Pink chenille
- Hackle: Shell Pink saddle
- Rib: Gold wire

Tied by Ralph Kanz

POPPER, FOAM OR HARD BODY

They're meant to splash, pop, chug, and sputter. These flies should push water and create a real disturbance when you animate them.

Using a full floating line, work the fly with a series of short rapid strips, letting the popper pause on occasion. Use your rod tip to redirect the fly's course.

Striped bass and surface-roaming rockfish will pound the fly. Poppers can provide some terrific action during a night bite.

Materials
- Hook: Saltwater, long shank, #2/0
- Thread: White
- Tail and Skirt: White, Black, or Yellow bucktail
- Body: Cork, foam, or balsa. Painted to suit if necessary.
- Eyes: Plastic doll (hollow or solid), peel-off prismatic or painted

Commercial production tie

PURPLE EELWORM

Dave Whitlock came up with this dynamite streamer. In the salt it's a great imitation for small eels, blennies, and marine worms. rockfish, cabezon, and greenling have all been caught with this pattern.

Use the fly on a sinking shooting head with a fairly short leader. Keep the eelworm crawling along the bottom. Fish it slow and easy.

Materials
- Hook: Salmon/Steelhead, #2–4
- Thread: Purple
- Weedguard: Hard nylon
- Eyes: Medium or large bead chain
- Tail: 2–4 slender Grizzly hackle dyed Purple, 3x shank length
- Body: Coarse dubbing, Purple
- Rib: Wide soft hackle, Grizzly-dyed Purple, palmered
- Head: Same as body

Fly Pattern Recipes and Angling Tips

SALTY SEAFOAM BLONDE

This pattern is a variation of the classic *Blonde Series* developed by Joe Brooks. Joe's "Blondes" were designed for striped bass, Salmon, and other top predator species.

Tied on larger hooks they'll work for stripers and rockfish. Smaller sized patterns tempt bonito and mackerel.

You can work the fly with any style line. It performs best from the surface to about thirty feet. Leader length will vary from three feet to approximately nine feet.

Use a subtle rod action as you strip-in the offering.

Materials
- Hook: Standard saltwater, #2–4/0
- Thread: White
- Tail: Layered, White and Blue bucktail, tied long
- Body: Flat Silver tinsel
- Underwing: Pearl Krystal Flash
- Wing: Layered, Green and Blue bucktail, tied long

SASQUATCH, DARK

The author's original concept was to imitate the fry of bass and trout. It also imitates sculpin and other tasty treats in the salty shallows. On experimenting in the field, the fly has taken rockfish and cabezon along the rocky shore.

It's a good general attractor used near the surface or at mid-depths. The fly works well in low light situations.

Materials
- Hook: Salmon/Steelhead, Gold, heavy wire, #1/0–4
- Thread: Yellow
- Tag: Silver tinsel thread
- Tail: Fluorescent Yellow floss, Pale Orange Krystal Flash
- Body: First half shank, Dark Brown sparkle chenille
- Underwing: Fluorescent Yellow floss
- Body: Second half shank, Lite Brite Gold, apply with dub loop
- Collar: Teal flank, Natural

SCREAMIN' (SHAD) SHRIMP

Brett Jensen had Shad in mind when he designed his original pattern. Little did he know it would become such an outrageous success for surfperch, mackerel, topsmelt, and salmon!

Use the fly on a sink tip or sinking shooting head with a medium length leader. A short snapping and darting style retrieve gets interest.

Materials
- Hook: Standard Saltwater, #2–6
- Thread: Fluorescent Fire Orange
- Tail/Antennae: White bucktail
- Eyes: Medium bead chain
- Rib: Gold wire
- Carapace: Pale Orange Krystal Flash
- Overbody: Clear "V-Rib" or substitute
- Body: Tying thread

Fly Pattern Recipes and Angling Tips

SHAD FLY, SILVER /RED

Tied by the author

The Shad Fly can be used to imitate fry, baitfish, or the roe sac of sand crabs. It's really just a general attractor.

The pattern will often draw strikes from surfperch, mullet, mackerel, croaker, and bonito.

You can work the fly with any style line, usually at fairly shallow depths. It performs best in the surfline and protected coves.

Materials
- Hook: Heavy wire, Silver, #2–6
- Thread: White or Red
- Eyes: Medium bead chain
- Tail: White or Red hackle fibers
- Body: Silver mylar tinsel
- Collar: Red chenille
- Hackle: White

SURFPERCHER RED

Tied by John Shewey

A John Shewey design for (you guessed it) surfperch. This fly cuts through the pounding surf easily. The marabou looks lively, with the red and yellow color used as a trigger to imitate crab roe.

Using a sink tip or sinking shooting head (leader length will vary), work the fly along the sandy bottom. John often uses this pattern on a dropper rig, with a simple streamer as the lead fly.

Materials
- Hook: Standard Saltwater, #4–1/0
- Thread: Red
- Tail: Yellow marabou tips
- Body: Gold diamond braid
- Throat: Yellow marabou
- Wing: Red marabou, topped with Red Flashabou
- Eyes: Bead chain, or lead barbell if used in heavy/deep surf

WAYFARER

Tied by the author

Created by the author, this slice of life in the salty foodchain tempts such species as bonito, mackerel, and rockfish. Use it as a general attractor, especially when the fish are finicky eaters.

Use the fly on a floating or intermediate head with a medium length leader. Short strips in a darting retrieve work well. Keep the fly shallow.

Materials
- Hook: Salmon/Steelhead, Gold, heavy wire, #2–4
- Tag: Green Antron yarn
- Tail: Green Antron yarn
- Butt: Lite Brite, Pearl blue
- Body: Lite Brite Yellow
- Underwing: Peacock Krystal Flash
- Wing and beard: Green Antron yarn
- Collar: Teal flank, Natural

From bottom-to-to
a list of *best b*

California Coast Crab
Pacific Rock Crab
Oregon Cancer Crab
Pacific Mole Crab
Various Porcelain Crabs
… and tons of crab larvae!

Beach Ghost Shrimp
Bay Ghost Shrimp
Coon-Stripe Shrimp
Krill
Marine Worms

7–8 weight outfits recommended when targeting these species.

Corbina

Jack Smelt

Striped Mullet

Mackeral

Herring

Opaleye

Yellowtail Croaker

Sargo

Barred Surfperch

n the foodchain, here's
dibles to emulate.

Sculpin
Plainfin Midshipman
Blennie
Eel

Pacific Herring
Pacific Sardine
Various Silversides
Northern Anchovy
Candlefish
Striped Mullet
Mackerel

Various Gamefish Young

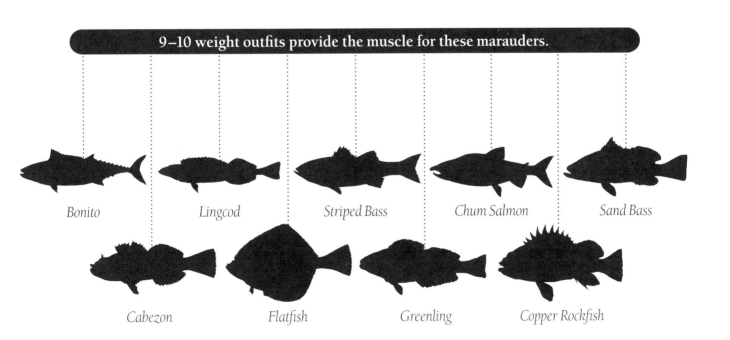

9–10 weight outfits provide the muscle for these marauders.

Bonito   *Lingcod*   *Striped Bass*   *Chum Salmon*   *Sand Bass*

Cabezon   *Flatfish*   *Greenling*   *Copper Rockfish*

Equipment for the Salty Flyrodder Afoot

My first saltwater "outfit" included a dirt-cheap fiberglass rod, a dinged-up entry-level Pflueger reel, hand-me-down DT floating fly line, a few split shot sinkers, and a mess of scraggly ol' steelhead bugs. It wasn't much to look at, but it got me into some fish. Over time, I upgraded the outfit and expanded my coastal adventures. Fishing demanding habitat and tangling with larger, exotic species, became a reality with better performance tackle. The quality of the gear you choose will definitely dictate the limits of your surf zone pursuits. It's not a matter of finances… it's a matter of equipment integrity and realistic field applications. Your equipment needn't be expensive. The equipment does however, need to be reliable!

When it comes to equipment design, take a straight forward practical approach to assembling your gear. For most of us that translates into modifying outfits we already have. It's not that difficult to make the jump to shoreline fly fishing. During your freshwater forays have you been casting to coastal steelhead or lunker Largemouth Bass? If so, you probably own an outfit that's perfect for trying a salty shoreline adventure!

This guidebook isn't the place for an in-depth discussion of equipment design or production techniques. There are plenty of resources devoted specifically for that. Instead, use the guidebook as a reference tool for basic rod-reel-line selections, and ancillary gear that will help you safely and effectively pursue this sensational arena for fly fishing.

PHOTO BY AUTHOR

Rods and Reels

You'll be choosing an outfit tailored toward the environment, rather than a particular species. Heavy hydraulics and thick salty cover can play havoc with timid tackle. The overwhelming majority of your work should be with rods ranging within the 7–10 weight categories. A survey among my colleagues shows that the outift that reigns supreme, "the Pacific wand," is a 9'/9-weight. You'll find times when a lighter rod will be perfect, and days (or nights) when a heavier blank might be preferred, but not everyone can enjoy the benefits of owning multiple saltwater outfits. Hedge your bet toward a nine weight blank and you'll get a big bang for your buck.

Look for a strong butt section in the rod blank's design. This primary feature will add the power to manage repeated long distance casts, and play an important role in fighting any fish around heavy cover and structure. Ideally, you want a blank that loads and dampens quickly. Both features enhance your ability to cast tighter loops, helping to deliver any size fly into biting coastal winds.

The use of oversized guides (notably the tip top and stripping guides) amplify line casting and retrieve qualities. Larger diameter guides allow for free-running line without snagging knots and rigging.

Saltwater and sand can destroy a reel overnight. It's up to you to maintain the integrity of your reel's original design features. Don't expect a poorly maintained reel to stop a bulldogging Lingcod, or protect your tippet from a hot running Bonito.

In today's market, most any reel can be used on a shoreline adventure. Just adhere to a consistent cleaning and maintenance schedule each time you expose your gear to the effects of saltwater. If you wish to upgrade to a true "saltwater design" look for deep anodized surfaces (corrosion protection), a smooth-running drag system, and be sure the bearings and inner works are sealed for extra protection.

No matter which reel design you use, allow enough capacity to carry at least 150 yards of backing (20 pound test minimum). If you venture after speedsters like striped bass or bonito, you should have at least 250 yards of backing. Most inshore species won't spool your line, but just the same, it would be advantageous to prepare for the unexpected.

Lines

Line designs are one of the most under-appreciated aspects of the fly fishing game. Every fly fisher carries a dizzying array of flies into the field, but how many of you own more than a standard floating flyline? Now don't get me wrong, I don't advocate carrying "a dizzying array of lines" into the field. However, consider the advantages that a sinking-style line provides. Sinking lines cut through the thick salty medium and present your offering anywhere, from inches subsurface, to dredging the bottom. Since most of the predators feed on free-roaming baitfish or crawling crustaceans, you'll want to put the fly where the fish is willing to eat it!

There are four unique categories for sinking style lines; Sink Tip, Full Sinking, Uniform Sink, and Sinking Shooting Heads. Each of the four styles has its strong points. Expect each line to perform at an optimum level in the proper field situation.

Sink Tip lines are really two lines in one. The heavy tip delivers the fly below the surface while, at the same time, you enjoy all the advantages of a floating belly section. The floating section is often used to track the fly's progress and can be an effective strike indicator in deeper water. Mending your line on the surface and preparing for the next cast becomes a breeze with the floating section. Sink tips vary from five to thirty feet in length. Take into account the water characteristics, gamefish, and fly selection before you commit yourself to a tip length. Typically the shorter tips are used for extremely shallow water applications and delivering smaller fly patterns. The longer tips are designed for deep water, large flies, and heavy hydraulics.

Full Sinking lines keep your offering in the strike zone longer. When you animate the fly, it doesn't tend to swing or jump toward the surface. Instead, you can creep and crawl the bugger down among the kelp and rocks for an extended presentation each retrieve cycle.

The Uniform Sink is actually an improvement on full-sinking lines. It incorporates a graduated-density construction technique that allows the tip to sink a bit faster than the belly of the line. This style line doesn't exhibit any "line sag". Your fly tracks better, improving fingertip strike and depth control.

Sinking Shooting Heads allow you the freedom to change your line instantly. Using a loop-to-loop system on your running line, exchange the head from a slow sinker (200 grains) to a super-fast sink (500+ grains) and keep on fishing! Shooting heads are superb for long distance casting situations. They're typically available in lengths of twenty-four to thirty feet.

The fishing industry uses two systems to categorize the sink rate of any specific line. One system simply describes the sinking quality with the following titles: Slow, Medium, Fast, Very Fast (or Extra Fast), and Ultra Fast (or Super Fast). It's certainly not the most scientific terminology, but we get a pretty good picture of what the line will do in the water. The second system is much more exact, based on drop ratings of *inches per second*. The actual "IPS rating" varies depending on the length of the sinking tip, or if the line is a full or uniform sinking style. The sink rates generally vary from one and a half inches per second, to more than eight inches per second.

So which rating is the best? If you use just one line, you're probably safe choosing a style rated between five to eight inches per second, or labeled "very fast" or "ultra fast." By varying your retrieve technique, you can control how fast (and how far) the line actually sinks the offering.

"Gadgets" and Other Stuff

Any flyfisher worth his salt has a compilation of accessories bordering on absurdity. Scanning through the mass of gadgets there are a few gems in every collection. For example, let's take the simple hook hone, or your polarized sunglasses. Both items deserve to be elevated from accessory to "essential" status.

Here are three noteworthy items to assist you in gear maintenance, field technique, and personal safety:

One of the most valuable contraptions you can carry into the field is an "all-in-one tool." The Leatherman Tool is a fine example of what a well-crafted multi-use implement provides: solid stainless steel construction, needlenose pliers, regular pliers, wire and line cutters, knife blade, a variety of screwdrivers, the list goes on. There are probably numerous uses you can come up with to justify this tool's place in your tackle collection. Here are a few:

- Pliers add grip when working with heavy monofilament

- Wire cutters help handle wire "shock tippets"
- Screwdriver for reel maintenance
- The tool helps with "catch-and-release" keeping fingers away from toothy creatures

Stripping baskets are becoming a popular accessory in the saltwater realm. This is one of those items you'll either love or hate. Have you ever considered using a stripping basket to help with line control and casting technique? Generally worn around your waste, the basket can catch coils of line as you retrieve your fly. The loosely coiled line is kept free from debris and wave surge, allowing for unencumbered running line as you initiate your next casting stroke. Baskets are a great choice for rocky shores and jetty journeys. In some wading environs, like the Pacific Northwest, they're less than ideal in the rougher surf. As long as you're wading within a relatively calm arena, the stripping basket can contribute to your field success.

The classic rain poncho is another multi-use item for the salty flyrodder afoot. It protects you from the elements and is a super ground cover for control on the rocks. As a dropcloth, the poncho can help eliminate line snags and tangles. It's a fast and easy alternative to a stripping basket.

Clothing

Your choice of clothing has a great deal to do with your success, comfort, and safety seaside. The Pacific's glorious coastline, from steep-sloping beachheads to vast gentle flats, requires that your clothing be as adaptable as your field techniques and tackle.

When jumping around rocks or prowling jetties and breakwaters, I still opt for "basic outdoorwear." My boots are a simple hiking design. They provide solid support, protect against abrasion, and help keep my feet warm. Occasionally I'll incorporate the use of Korkers. The character of the rock can be highly polished, feeling like a greased pane of glass, or it might be a bit "gravely" giving the sensation of walking on mini-marbles. Add a few well-placed carpets of brown algae, sea grass, colonies of mussels and you can see where this begins to become tricky footing.

Loose-fitting items give me the freedom to move with greater ease among the rocks. My pants are usually a rugged cotton canvas. In this slippery, rocky domain, I often choose not to wear waders. My single most important garment might well be a windproof/water-repellent shell. It provides great protection during potential hypothermic conditions. As an extra measure, I definitely keep a change of clothes in the truck!

Keeping in mind that everyone will ultimately refine their own "uniform" based on home waters, wading skills, seasons, etc., consider that you'll be dealing with salt and sand invasion, potential undertows, and lots of the wet stuff!

If you find yourself having to wade in the surf, or an estuary, consider water temperature, currents, tide and terrain qualities. Most often you'll be standing ankle- or knee-deep in the foam. A more aggressive approach

Think "safety first!" Fish with a partner and wear the proper protective clothing.   PHOTO BY AUTHOR

might have you facing-off with pounding breakers! *Only you can determine if the risk is worth entering* when the sea "exposes its ugly side."

Neoprene is probably the safest material on the market today. Its ability to insulate and float, is a prime reason for using it in the ocean realm. On a scale of 1 to 10, it rates 10+ for use in cold weather, rough sea, or unstable conditions.

Most freshwater flyfishers cross over to the salty surf wearing their "Weinbrenner" or "Cordura style" wading shoes, and chest high stocking foot neoprenes. Stop! Save your shoes! The salt 'n sand is insidious stuff! The salt is abusive on the lacing system and any other metal. (What about Velcro designs? Trust me on this one… they don't work well out here.) If adhesives are used on the sole, repeatedly exposing them to salt can weaken the bond. Sand entering the shoe becomes abrasive on the footbed as well as against the neoprene stocking foot. Stitching is susceptible to any grating affect. Remember, you're not wading in a streambed, the currents aren't just flowing past you. The surf zone is a unique environment with its

heavy hydraulics, and not well suited for this type of boot.

By switching to a simple neoprene *flats bootie*, or a dive bootie, you will have a much more effective outfit. The top of the bootie creates a tighter seal around your ankle. There's less sand entering the footbed. Add an inexpensive gravel cuff and you've really got a dynamite solution. With little or no metal in the bootie's design, maintenance is kept to a minimum. Their lightweight design is a real plus if you're required to swim to shore.

If you plan on spending a great deal of time pursuing this sport, and it finds you in colder/rougher conditions, consider using a "boot-foot wader." It's a beautiful solution to completely stopping sand and salt invasion. Plus, you get the added bonus of having a *no-catch zone* around your legs. Without laces and extra cuffs, you're less likely to have your line coiled and confused around your shoes.

Whether you use neoprene waders, poly/nylon lightweights, or rubber/nylon mid-weight designs, *be sure to use a wading belt.* You can't imagine how much of a safety margin this

creates. Ask anyone that's taken a dunking while wearing one! I'm sure they can vouch for it's effectiveness. There's no excuse for not having this feature. A belt is smart insurance!

Using a jacket to cover your waders is a great idea. I recommend a simple pullover style with a hood. Be sure the design allows a tight seal around the waist. Shedding water and insulating you from freight-train wind blasts are two great benefits of the garment. Most importantly, it inhibits water from flooding your waders if you lose your footing.

In a warmer, gentler environment, you still have to deal with saltwater, sand, wind, and sun. I prefer to wear clothes that reduce windchill, allow freedom of movement, and require little post-event care.

Foot care is of primary concern. Personally I don't like wading in sandals. I prefer the extra safety of a fully-enclosed bootie design. For a warm weather version of the neoprene bootie, consider the low-cut profile on Nike's "Aqua Turf" footwear. The upper is made of a 4-way stretch mesh Spandex, the tight-fitting collar is neoprene, and the slipper sports a rugged wrap-around outsole for extra protection. Combined with ultralight waders, or long nylon pants, this provides ample protection and insulation.

A final thought on your clothing system… consider using eye protection. A hat with a wide brim adds to the effectiveness of polarized glasses, while at the same time protecting you from "less than ideal" casting technique.

A Word About Knots & Rigging

You can get into a ton of trouble by taking knots for granted! In pursuit of salty gamefish we often find our flies being bounced, bonked, and otherwise abused by semi-hostile surroundings. The tumultuous surfline can grind your knot into smithereens. A tricky kelpbed can trap the fly in a convolution of debris. Shoreline fly fishing is truly a time to pay close attention to your terminal tackle.

As fly fishers, we can't control water conditions or master the weather. Nor do we reign over any fish's behavior. When it comes down to it, there are just a few things we really do have dominion over. Knot selection and tying execution is clearly an aspect of the sport where we can exercise a great deal of control.

Taking a few extra seconds when tying on your fly can be the difference between a triumphant portrait or maddening knot failure. There's really no excuse for knot failure. There's a myriad of specialty knots for just about any fishing application you can think of. Balancing your rigging to match both species and habitat, is just as critical as choosing the right pattern to represent a school of baitfish or imitate a crab.

Two knots of particular note are the *Duncan Loop* and *Palomar Knot* designs. One adds to the lively presentation of any streamer, while the other's tenacious grip enables you to go just about anywhere you darn well please!

Step One: *Thread your tippet through the eye. Give yourself plenty of line to manipulate the knot in progress. Bend the tag back toward the hook. You've just created an elongated "S" (basically it's two loops side-by-side).*

Step Two: *Using the tag end of your tippet, wrap five turns around the two lines that create the top loop. You'll be passing through the bottom loop with each turn of the tag end.*

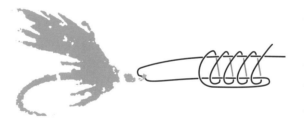

Step Three: *Slowly pull on the tag to walk the knot in place. Just before you secure the knot, slide it to create the desired size loop you wish to work with. Larger sized loops will allow an exaggerated side-to-side swinging motion during a slow or medium retrieve. Smaller loops create a more stunted pattern, best used during a rapid retrieve cycle.*

The Duncan Loop is a great way to induce a bit more life into your streamers or poppers, while at the same time protecting your tippet with a built-in shock absorbing feature. The design's loop will allow your fly to swing freely while you puppeteer the pattern. Once a gamefish smacks the offering, the knot slips down to a more secure position near the hook's eye. The knot's "slipping action" absorbs the initial impact of the strike, dissipating pressure and protecting lighter tippets from sudden failure.

Big fish and nasty habitat can put a "world of hurt" on your terminal tackle. The extra effort you put forth in selecting a knot, and then taking the time to tie it correctly, can have a dramatic effect on your success. Check frequently for any signs of abrasion or potential failure. Re-tie, or upgrade the knot as many times as is necessary to keep control of the situation. You're just a cast away from a "thrill-a-minute!"

Rigging

Terminal tackle designs can often find specialized sections for the leader butt, class tippet, and shock trace. If you're out to pursue a record-breaking catch there are strict guidelines to adhere to. The *International Game Fish Association* can provide you with the specifics. Another valuable resource for rigging designs is Lefty Kreh and Mark Sosin's *Practical Fishing Knots*. Their book presents over fifty different knot designs and various formulas for both fresh and saltwater leaders.

If you choose to work with a "basic" system, your foundation will be a butt section (30 pound mono recommended) of approximately two to four feet in length. You can vary the butt using the short version for deep-water applications, and a slightly longer version for shallow-water techniques. A simple straight tippet (approximately 12 pound test) can then be attached. Again, you can vary the tippet's length, generally from two to six feet overall. This is a straight-forward system that can give you the necessary muscle to explore our western inshore fisheries.

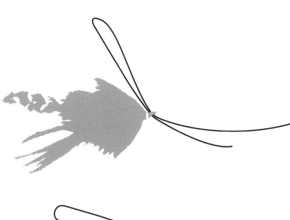

Step One: *Start by taking the tag end of your tippet and creating a bend in it. Don't be afraid to use a bit of material here. It's easier to work the knot if you give yourself some extra monofilament to manipulate. Pass half the double line through the eye of the hook.*

Step Two: *Using the double line, tie a basic overhand knot, keep the circle open. You should now have the hook's eye trapped within the overhand knot. Be sure to tie the overhand so as to leave yourself a loop at the end of the double line. At the hook's bend, run the loop over the back of the shank.*

Step Three: *Hold the hook in one hand, while at the same time pulling on the standing/tag line with the other hand. A moderate, steady pressure will begin walking the knot into place. As the overhand knot draws down behind the eye, be sure to let the "walking loop" travel down the shank and over the eye to trap the overhand knot before tightening. Properly executed this knot can test from 95–100% breaking strength. It's one tough bugger!*

The Palomar Knot is a superb choice for working swimming streamers or bottom-bouncing some furry mime. It offers a secure grip on any style hook eye. It's a "hard knock" knot, exhibiting a great deal of strength when it comes to abrasion resistance. The knot incorporates double the tippet material passing through the hook's eye, and a nifty lockdown feature to finish the design. It's simple to tie (OK, OK, I know you've heard that before but at least give this one a try).

WASHINGTON

Mukkaw Bay
Ruby Beach
Beach #3
South Beaches
Hood Canal Area
Pacific Beach State Park
Westhaven/Westport
Long Beach
McKenzie Head • Pacific Pines State Park

LOCATION	HABITAT			
	Sandy Shore	Rocky Shore	Bay/Estuary	Jetty/Pier
Hood Canal Area Eagle Creek			oyster beds, shallow estuary	
Hoodsport			oyster beds, shallow estuary	
Chico Creek			oyster beds, shallow estuary	
Potlatch Park			oyster beds, shallow estuary	
Mukkaw Bay	moderate slope, remote, miles long			
Olympic Nat. Park Ruby Beach	moderate slope, good road access	seastacks nearby		
Beach #3	mild/mod. slope, good road access	tidepools, rocky cove		
South Beaches	moderate slope, good road access	tidepools		
Pacific Beach State Park	wide, mild slope, drive-on access			
Westhaven/ Westport	wide, mild slope		estuary, Grays Harbor	
Long Beach	long spit, drive-on access			
McKenzie Head				jetty
Pacific Pines State Park	wide, mild slope			

OREGON

Columbia River Jetties
Seaside
Nehalem Bay S.P.
Bayocean Peninsula
Cape Lookout State Park • Tillamook Area
Siletz Bay
Newport Area
Seal Rock
Oregon Dunes
Winchester Bay
Coos Bay Area
Port Orford
Brookings Area

LOCATION	HABITAT			
	Sandy Shore	Rocky Shore	Bay/Estuary	Jetty/Pier
Columbia River Jetties			estuary	jetties
Seaside	mild slope	sporadic rocks		
Nehalem Bay State Park	long spit, mild slope		bay, Nehalem	jetty
Bayocean Peninsula	long spit, moderate slope		bay, Tillamook	jetty
Cape Lookout State Park	long spit, moderate slope		bay, Netarts	
Tillamook Area	long spit, moderate slope		bay, Tillamook	jetty
Siletz Bay	mild slope, strong currents		natural estuary	
Newport Area	moderate slope, south side of beach		bay, Yaquina	jetty
Seal Rock	moderate/steep, heavy surf	seastacks, pocket pools		
Oregon Dunes	mild/mod slope, very remote			
Winchester Bay			estuary, Umpqua/Smith River	
Coos Bay Area			bay/estuary	jetty
Port Orford	steep slope, narrow	pocket pools, headlands		
Brookings Area	steep slope, narrow	pocket pools	estuary, Chetco River	jetty

LOCATION	SPECIES					
	Surfperch	**Rockfish**	**Lingcod**	**Misc. Salmon**	**Cabezon**	**Greenling**
Hood Canal Chico Creek				Falll		
Potlatch Park				Fall		
Hoodsport				Fall		
Eagle Creek				Fall		
Mukkaw Bay	May – September	all year				
Olympic Nat. Park Ruby Beach	May – September	all year				Fall
Beach #3	May – September	all year				Fall
South Beaches	May – September	all year				Fall
Pacific Beach State Park	March – September					
Westhaven/ Westport	May – September	all year	Winter	Fall	Winter	Fall/Win/Spr
Long Beach	April – September					
McKenzie Head		all year	Winter		Fall/Winter	Fall
Pacific Pines State Park	March – September					

LOCATION	SPECIES					
	Surfperch	**Rockfish**	**Ling/Cab**	**Misc. Salmon**	**Striped Bass**	**Greenling**
Columbia River Jetties	all year	all year	all year	Spring/Fall		all year
Seaside	May – September	all year				
Nehalem Bay State Park	April – September	all year	Winter	Fall		Winter
Bayocean Peninsula	April – September	all year	Winter			Winter
Cape Lookout State Park	April – September	all year				
Tillamook Area	April – September	all year	Winter/Spring	Fall		all year
Siletz Bay	March – June		Winter/Spring	Fall		
Newport Area	April – September	all year	Winter/Spring	Fall		all year
Seal Rock	April – June	all year	all year			all year
Oregon Dunes	April – September					
Winchester Bay	April – September	all year	Winter	Fall	June – October	all year
Coos Bay Area	April – September	all year	Winter	Fall	June – October	all year
Port Orford	April – September	all year	Winter		Winter	all year
Brookings Area	May – September	all year	Winter	Fall	Winter	Winter

Map labels (north to south):
- Kellogg Road Beach
- Crescent Bay Area
- Trinidad State Beach
- Mad River Beach
- North/South Spits • Humbolt Bay Area
- MacKerricher State Park
- Noyo Harbor Area
- Big River
- Fish Rock Beach
- Goat Rock Beach
- Salmon Creek
- Dillon Beach
- Duxbury Reef
- Ocean Beach
- Rockaway Beach • Sharp Park Beach
- James Fitzgerald
- Pillar Point Harbor
- East Breakwater
- Pescadero and Gazos Creek State Beaches • San Gregorio State Beach
- Natural Bridges State Beach
- Sunset State Beach

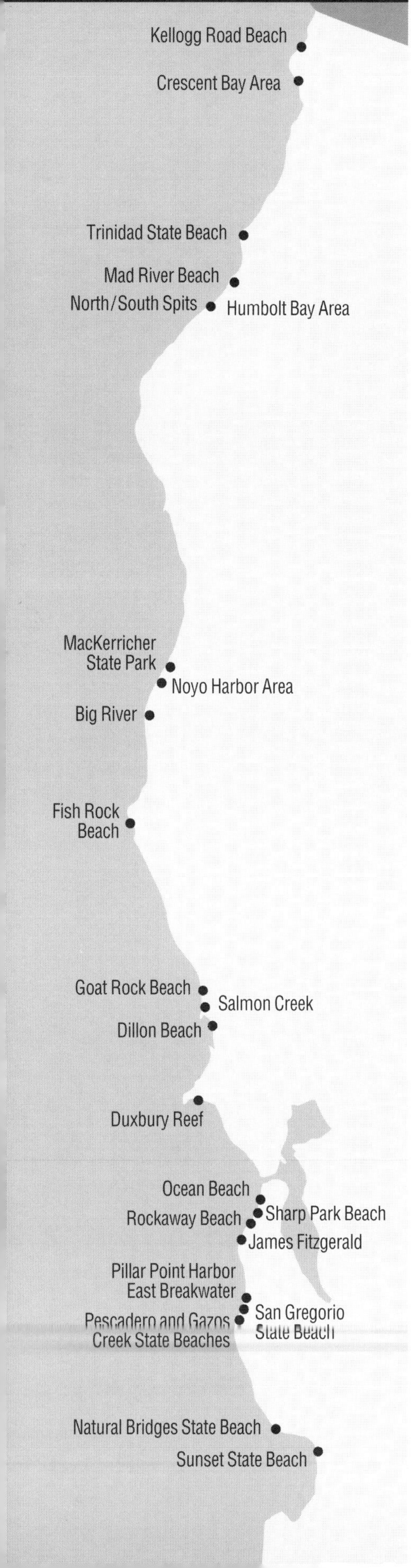

LOCATION	HABITAT			
	Sandy Shore	Rocky Shore	Bay/Estuary	Jetty/Pier
Kellogg Road Beach	moderate slope, wide	sporadic rock		
Crescent Bay Area				jetty
Trinidad State Beach	moderate slope, wide	headlands		
Mad River Beach	moderate slope, protected cove		estuary	
North Spit	long spit, good road access			jetty
South Spit			bay, Humboldt	jetty
MacKerricher State Park	mod/steep slope, extensive beach	sporadic rocks pocket pools		
Noyo Harbor	moderate slope, small			jetty
Big River			estuary	
Garcia River Access			estuary	
Fish Rock Beach	moderate slope	seastacks, tidepools		
Goat Rock Beach	moderate slope	seastacks	estuary, Russian River	
Salmon Creek	moderate slope, heavy surf	seastacks, sporadic rocks		
Dillon Beach	moderate slope, privately owned			
Duxbury Reef		headlands, tidepools		
Ocean Beach	moderate slope, heavy surf			
Sharp Park Beach	moderate slope			pier
Rockaway Beach	moderate slope, narrow			
James Fitzgerald	sheltered cove	finger reefs, tidepools		
Pillar Point Harbor			estuary	pier/jetty
East Breakwater			estuary	jetty
San Gregorio State Beach	moderate slope, sheltered cove	sporadic rocks, pocket pools		
Pescadero State Beach	moderate slope, wide	sporadic rocks,	estuary	
Gazos Creek State Beach	mod/steep slope, narrow	sporadic rocks, pocket pools		
Natural Bridges State Beach	mod/steep slope	tide pools, terraced cliffs		
Sunset State Beach	mod/steep slope			

LOCATION	SPECIES					
	Surfperch	**Rockfish**	**Lingcod**	**Misc. Salmon**	**Cabezon**	**Greenling**
Kellogg Road Beach	March – September					
Crescent Bay Area	March – September	all year				Winter
Trinidad State Beach	March – September	all year				
Mad River Beach	March – September					
North Spit	May – September	May – September				

LOCATION	**Surfperch**	**Rockfish**	**Striped Bass**	**Misc. Salmon**	**Flounder**	**Ling/Cab**
South Spit	March – September	all year			Winter	Winter
MacKerricher State Park	March – September	all year				
Noyo Harbor	March –September	all year		Fall	Winter	
Big River	March – September			Fall	Winter	
Garcia River Access	March – September			Fall/Winter		
Fish Rock Beach	March – September	all year				
Goat Rock Beach	March – September	all year				
Salmon Creek	March – September	all year				
Dillon Beach	March – September					
Duxbury Reef		all year				Winter
Ocean Beach	March – September		Summer			
Sharp Park Beach	March – September	all year	Summer			
Rockaway Beach	March – September	all year	Summer			
James Fitzgerald	all year	all year				Winter
Pillar Point Harbor	all year	all year				
East Breakwater	all year	all year				
San Gregorio State Beach	March – September	all year				

LOCATION	**Surfperch**	**Rockfish**	**Cabezon**	**Corbina**	**Croaker**	**Flounder**
Pescadero State Beach	March – September	all year	Winter		all year	Winter
Gazos Creek State Beach	March – September	all year	Winter			
Natural Bridges State Beach	March – October	all year	Winter			
Sunset State Beach	March – October					

Moss Landing Area
Asilomar State Beach
Carmel River State Beach
Marina State Beach
Andrew Molera
Hearst Memorial State Beach
Cayucos Beach
Pismo State Beach
Rancho Guadalupe
Jalama Beach
Gaviota State Park
Goleta Beach
Ledbetter Beach
Carpenteria State Park
San Buenaventura
McGrath State Beach
Channel Island Harbor
Leo Carillo State Beach
Kings Harbor
Redondo State Beach
Huntington State Beach
Newport Bay
Oceanside
San Elijo State Beach
Del Mar
Torrey Pines State Beach
Ocean Beach and Coronado Shores

LOCATION	HABITAT			
	Sandy Shore	**Rocky Shore**	**Bay/Estuary**	**Jetty/Pier**
Moss Landing State Beach	mod/steep slope, wide		estuary, Bennett Slough	jetty
Moss Landing Harbor			estuary, Elkhorn Slough	jetty
Marina State Beach	moderate slope			
Asilomar State Beach	moderate slope, narrow	sporadic rocks, pocket pools		
Carmel River State Beach	mild/mod slope	sporadic rocks		
Andrew Molera	mild slope, sheltered cove	headlands, steep cliffs	estuary, Big Sur River	
Hearst Memorial State Beach	mild/mod slope, sheltered			pier
Cayucos Beach	mild/mod slope			
Pismo State Beach	mild/mod slope, extensive beach			pier
Rancho Guadalupe	mild/mod slope			
Jalama Beach	mild/mod slope			
Gaviota State Park	mild/mod slope			pier
Goleta Beach	mild/mod slope			pier
Ledbetter Beach	wide, mild slope, shallow cove			
Carpenteria State Park	mild slope, narrow, shallow			
San Buenaventura	wide, mild slope, sheltered			pier
McGrath State Beach	mild slope			
Channel Island Harbor			estuary	jetty
Leo Carillo State Beach	mild slope, sheltered	tidepools, sporadic rocks		
Kings Harbor			estuary	jetty/pier
Redondo State Beach	mild slope			
Huntington State Beach	mild slope, wide			pier
Newport Bay				jetty
Oceanside	mild slope			pier
San Elijo State Beach	mild slope			
Del Mar	wide, mild slope, miles long			
Torrey Pines State Beach	mild slope			
Ocean Beach	mild slope			pier
Coronado Shores	mild slope			

LOCATION	SPECIES					
	Surfperch	**Rockfish**	**Cabezon**	**Corbina**	**Croaker**	**Flounder**
Moss Landing State Beach	March – October	all year			all year	Winter
Moss Landing Harbor	all year		Winter		all year	Winter
Marina State Beach	March – October					
Asilomar State Beach	March – October	all year	Winter			
Carmel River State Beach	March – October		Winter			
Andrew Molera	March – October	all year			all year	
Hearst Memorial State Beach	March – October				all year	Winter
Cayucos Beach	March – October					
Pismo State Beach	March – October				Summer	
Rancho Guadalupe	March – October					
Jalama Beach	March – October	all year				
Gaviota State Park	March – October		Winter	Summer		
Goleta Beach	March – October		Winter	Summer		
	Surfperch	**Sand Bass**	**Corbina**	**Croaker**	**Bonito**	**Bottomfish**
Ledbetter Beach	March – October	Summer	Summer	Summer		all year
Carpenteria State Park	March – October	Summer	Summer			
San Buenaventura	all year			Summer		
McGrath State Beach	all year		Summer	Summer		
Channel Island Harbor		Summer			Summer	
Leo Carillo State Beach	all year	Summer			Summer	Summer
Kings Harbor					Winter/Spring	
Redondo State Beach	all year		Summer			
Huntington State Beach	all year		Summer			
Newport Bay		Summer		Summer	Winter/Spring	
Oceanside	all year	Spring/Summer	Summer	Spring/Summer		
San Elijo State Beach	all year			Spring/Summer		
Del Mar	all year			Spring/Summer		
Torrey Pines State Beach	all year			Spring/Summer		
Ocean Beach	all year		Summer	Spring/Summer		
Coronado Shores	all year		Summer	Spring/Summer		

A Guide to Northern Baja's Pacific Coast

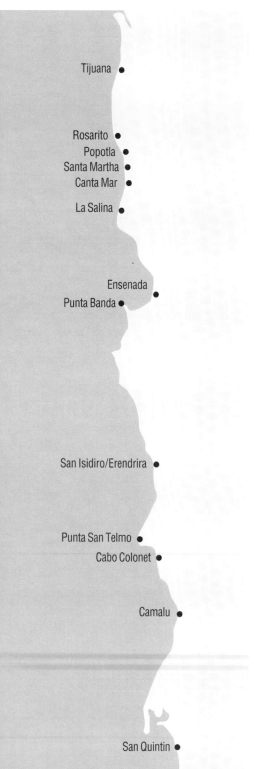

Tijuana

Rosarito
Popotla
Santa Martha
Canta Mar

La Salina

Ensenada
Punta Banda

San Isidiro/Erendrira

Punta San Telmo
Cabo Colonet

Camalu

San Quintin

Greg Jones and I had just passed through the Border Patrol's inspection post. The trip was officially over. We were back in the good ol' U.S. of A. What a trip it was, with three days of non-stop fishing from sun-up to sun-down, and at times continuing right into the night. We ran into a few local anglers, occasionally shared a beach with some touristas, but usually had the place to ourselves. There was never a lack of casting room, and mile after mile of surf, sand, and rocky shoreline to explore. It was pure heaven for a couple of surf-busters from the north. We had little problem finding fish that would bump, inhale, or attack our fly.

Pop over our southern border and you've just entered a paradise for saltwater flyfishers. A mere few-hour jaunt puts you into what's virtually one of the largest untapped resources on the Pacific Coast. Baja's northern beaches are rich with aquatic life. Their collection of gamefish is a marvelous experience for the "light tackle" salty flyrodder.

One of the great joys of fly fishing is the unpredictable adventure in the field. Let me just say – "Baja is one great adventure!" I've been exploring the peninsula since the late '60s and it's still worth the price of admission. In all my years south of the border I've experienced only one negative encounter. For the most part, it's as safe as anywhere else I venture off to. The golden rule is simply to travel smart, stay sharp, and don't become a target for trouble.

As you might expect, Baja California has evolved with time. Expansion and modernization have modified the rules a bit. In some cases the change is a welcome surprise, such as the upgraded road conditions along Highway One. In other instances, such as beach access, the change might cause major frustration. This last point is notably true if you haven't done your homework first. Yet when the dust finally settles, it's still a grand stage for the fly – filled with opportunity and a fine place to introduce yourself to the fascinating realm of saltwater flyrodding.

Tackle Tips

The region offers excellent fishing from March through November. The winter months can be a bear. For the flyfisher afoot, the most common catches will include barred surfperch, calico and sand bass, cabezon, yellowfin croaker, silversides, and various rockfish. You'll also have the opportunity for sargo, opaleye, flatfish, and the California corbina.

I want to be clear in stating that Baja's piscatory treasures are indeed a wild bunch. They don't jump into your stripping basket, and they don't commit suicide on your hook! Be fully prepared to adapt your tackle and field techniques. We've enjoyed success with floating/sinking lines, as well as shooting head systems. The heavier shooting heads were dynamite off the rocks and around the kelp beds. The lighter lines were effective in shallow estuaries and the surfline.

The majority of the time you'll be presenting streamers with an active animated retrieve. The baitfish patterns usually vary in size from #1/0 to #2. The rest of the collection should incorporate smaller marine munchies ranging from #2 to #6. The Pacific's a wondrous place, with a highly complex foodchain, and that's to your advantage! When it comes to your fly tackle remember this cardinal rule, "If you didn't pack it, it doesn't exist

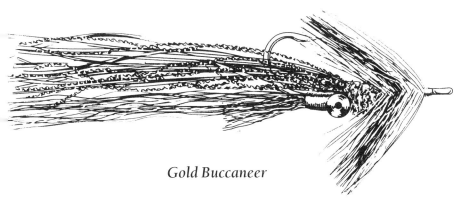

Gold Buccaneer

in Baja." It's better to carry too much than not enough.

Travel Options

Past winters have had a major effect on access roads throughout northern Baja. The torrential downpours washed out bridges, flooded towns, and literally obliterated secondary roads in some areas. Relief efforts have regained all of the highway access. As for the local "sedan roads," expect them to be rutted, pock marked, and in some cases marginal for two-wheel drive vehicles.

The explosion of resort developments has somewhat limited the access to a lot of beachfront property. While individual resorts can't restrict your use of a beach, they aren't required to provide public access through their grounds. Use their facility and gain instant access, or work a bit harder to circumvent the property lines. On the plus side, we'd found the fishing pressure to be non-existent on beaches around resorts (everyone's either playing tennis or snoozing near the swimming pool!). You can find a room in a resort for as little as $39 per night. If you wish to stay in a "four star" facility it will cost you approximately $80 – $100 per night.

RV travel has always been a big part of the tourist industry on the peninsula. Quality parks are easy to find. Their services generally run around $15 – $25 per night. One advantage to

frequenting these facilities is the emergency support they can provide a vehicle.

Cruisin' down in the VW bug? Pack your tent and sleeping bag. You can stay in a "basic" campground for as little as $3.50 per night. If you're the real adventuresome type, *free* camping locations become more realistic as you travel farther south. We found a super location near Punta San Telmo. The locals were terrific and the surfperch were smokin'.'

Local Characteristics

The fishing between Tijuana and Rosarito consists of rocky points, tidepools, and very small sandy coves. The beachhead tends to be more of a shingle style. That's to say, it's cobblestone in nature, with a slightly steeper face than the beaches farther south. Debris in the water could hinder your efforts in this region. In past outings, these northern beaches have produced some excellent catches.

Just south of Rosarito begins a stretch of beaches well worth investigating. The beachhead is less abrupt. The shingle style wanes as white sand begins to take hold. Sand crab colonies appear, and corbina can be seen cruising in the shallow surf. The flyfishing here can be awesome at times. Barred surfperch are a staple catch. Small lobster villages and fishing camps dot the coastline here. Puerto Nuevo is a must for anyone

with a taste for the rich crustacean and local brew. Popotla, Santa Martha, Canta Mar, all offer camping and lodging. Guides with fiberglass skiffs, known as "pangas", are available for hire. Rafts of kelp float just outside the breakers, loaded with opaleye and various gamefish.

The area adjacent to La Mision is a real winner for fly tackle. The beaches of Alisitos and La Salina are large, gorgeous, and prolific fishing grounds. Their white sands seem to go on forever. The sunsets here are supreme. The campground at Alisitos is convenient and clean. Hailing from the "La Mision Hotel," powerful flood lights send intense white beams into the Pacific's surfline each night. It's just the ticket for an extended flyfishing adventure! At La Salina you can drive your vehicle right onto the beach. Access is no problem.

Ensenada has always been a wild frontier town. It's no different today. The place is still colorful as they say. It's a booming trade center with a full service port of entry. You can hire local guides or prowl the beaches and estuary on foot. Between Ensenada and Maneadero, the protected waters of Bahia de Todos Santos are a potpourri for flyfishing. Located at the south end of the bay is the peninsula of Punta Banda. At the tip is La Bufadora, definitely our top pick for rocky shore and kelp bed activity. The species here will vary from calico bass to Spanish mackerel, cabezon, Pacific bonito, and various rockfish. Corbina and perch frequent the beachhead around La Jolla. Inside the estero you can catch sargo and croaker.

At Maneadero the highway turns inland and coastal access becomes very difficult. As you approach San Vicente, look for a small sign announcing the turnoff to Erendira. It's a secondary road (about twelve miles long) that most vehicles can negotiate. You can get lost in the maze of dirt roads, so be patient and head toward Castro's Fishing Place. There's opaleye, cabezon, calicos, and perch.

Heading back to the main highway and continuing south, Colonet is a good place to get gas, food, and various sundries. Access to San Antonio del Mar was washed out the last time I was in the area. If the sedan road has been repaired it's worth your while to explore the area. A short drive beyond Colonet is the junction for San Telmo.

Field References

Washington

Washington State Department of Fisheries

Main Office
115 General Administration Building
Olympia, WA 98504

Coastal Office
331 State Highway 12
Montesano, WA 98563

Washington State Parks and Recreation Commission
7150 Cleanwater Lane
Olympia, WA 98504

Oregon

Oregon Department of Fish and Wildlife

Main Office
2501 SW First Street
Portland, OR 97207

Northwest Office
7118 NE Vandenberg Ave.
Corvallis, OR 97330

Travel Documents and Stuff...

1. U.S. citizens are required to obtain a "Tourist Card" if you plan on staying more than 3 days in Baja, or if you will be travelling south of Ensenada. The cards are available in California at the Mexican Consulates. You can also apply at the Mexican Government Tourism Offices, or the immigration office at the border. There is no charge for the card. You'll need to provide either a passport, official birth certificate, or similar document to obtain the tourist card.

2. All vehicles should carry Mexican Auto Insurance. The cost is about $8 per day. Mexico requires that you carry vehicle registration papers.

3. Fishing licenses are available through the Mexico Department of Fisheries located in San Diego, or from "Oficinas de Pesca" in Baja.

Southwest Office
4192 N. Umpqua Highway
Roseburg, OR 97470

State of Oregon
Economic Development Department
Tourism Division, Parks and
Wilderness Areas
775 Summer Street NE
Salem, OR 97310

California

California Department of Fish and Game

Main Office
1416 9th Street
Sacramento, CA 94244

Region 1 Area
619 Second Street
Eureka, CA 95501

Region 3 Area
2201 Garden Road
Monterey, CA 93940

Turn *west*, and take the sedan road to Punta San Telmo and Cabo Colonet. There's superb surf action here for croaker and perch. The beach's character varies from cobblestone to black sand. The surrounding countryside is a wonderful mix of cactus and savannah.

I highly recommend that if you have the time, continue on to Camalu and ultimately the San Quintin region. It's series of estuary and bay waters, plus the sandy shoreline, offer spectacular opportunities for light tackle flyrodding.

Region 5 Area
330 Golden Shore, Suite #50
Long Beach, CA 90802

California Department of Parks and Recreation
PO Box 2390
Sacramento, CA 95811

Mexico

Mexico Department of Fisheries
2550 Fifth Ave., Suite 101
San Diego, CA 92103

State Secretary of Tourism of Baja California Norte
Centro Gobierno
Zona Rio Tijuana
Tijuana, BCN, Mexico

General Interest

Tidelog
Pacific Publishers
Box 480
Bolinas, CA 94924

*T*he West Coast is one of the longest uninterrupted coastlines on the planet. From the tip of Alaska to the tip of Baja is a few thousand miles as the crow flies. As measured by a cartographer, it is over 56,000 miles!
I have my secret places, now it's your turn to find some of your own.

LEFTY'S DECEIVER, OLIVE

PINK KEEL BUGGER

MINI PUFF

POPPER, FOAM OR HARD BODY

PEARL YETI

PURPLE EELWORM

PHILLIPS' KRAB KREATURE

SALTY SEAFOAM BLONDE